Words We Can Dance

Words We Can Dance

Thoughts for dance students, performers and teachers.

Francisco De La Calleja

She Dances With Him Productions

ISBN: 978-0-9959836-1-8

©2019 She Dances With Him Productions

First edition. All rights reserved.

No part of this book may be reproduced, stored in a retrieval system, or transmitted or broadcast in any form or by any means, electronic, mechanical, photocopying, sound or video recording or otherwise without the written permission of the publisher.

She Dances With Him Productions
PO Box 3301 Lapierre Station
LaSalle (Montréal), QC
H8N3N4
CANADA

Legal Deposit 2019
Library and Archives Canada
Bibliothèque Nationale du Québec

*To my first dance teacher,
Antonieta Cortés Bareño.
Your words were the first beat I learned to follow.*

Contents

Acknowledgements 9
How This Book Happened 10
Living 13
Learning 21
Performing 35
Teaching 49
Photo credits 70
About The Author 71

Acknowledgements

Inspiration has many sources. I would like to express my admiration and gratitude to thinkers and speakers of all walks of life such as Robert Fulghum, (cowboy, Unitarian minister, art teacher) Yogi Berra, Roger Staubach, Johan Cruyff, Emil Zatopek, (athletes) Henry Ford, (industrialist) Mark Twain, Wayne Dyer, Og Mandino, Nikos Kazantzakis, Dale Carnegie, (writers) Wilbur and Orville Wright, Richard Bach, Stephen Coonts, Antoine de Saint-Exupery, (airplane pilots), Barrett Tillman, (military historian) Serge Brosseau, (real estate broker) Jasmine Roy (actor) and Dr. Gordon Livingstone (psychologist).

None of them are or were dance teachers but their love for words inspires me to keep on learning how to speak, teach and motivate.

How This Book Happened

When I began taking dance lessons at age fifteen, my whole world changed. Dancing provided purpose and emphasis to my life. It gave me a sense of identity and accomplishment. I loved the way my teacher inspired me. I wanted to be like her.

So, shortly after my seventeenth birthday, I found employment at a ballroom dance studio that offered free teacher training with no experience required. At the time I expected this to be just a summer job.

But that fall, I did not return to school. I had become obsessed with the idea of becoming a good dance teacher.   I was spending a lot of time at the studio. I was new, so I wasn't teaching much. Instead, I trained with the other instructors, practiced a lot on my own, cleaned the mirrors, scrubbed the toilets, made the coffee, watched the other teachers teach and observed the professional dancers rehearse.

I left my parent's home and moved into a basement room in the house the directors of the studio rented in the outskirts of town. I wanted to spend my time with people who believed that teaching dance was a worthy and important career. I was living my dreams.

One morning we were all sitting in the kitchen drinking coffee. It was then that I saw it. One of the souvenir coffee mugs was covered in colorful writing. I got curious so I picked it up and read it. It was all dancing proverbs:

Shaw's *Stuff of Which Art Is Made*, Einstein's *Athletes of God*, Nureyev's *We Live because* and Nietzsche's *God That Could Dance*, among others.

It dawned on me that what had made my own dance teachers so good in my eyes was the way their words were memorable, like the proverbs on the mug. So, I made it part of my everyday work to avidly listen to and study every word my instructors and coworkers uttered.

After a while, I realized that I too, could come up with memorable phrases if I just observed the student's reactions to what I said, if I listened to myself a bit more carefully and especially if I spoke with the single-minded purpose of helping my students.

Weeks turned into months and the shy, stuttering teenager with the foreign accent that I was, slowly began to morph into a competent dancer, a confident communicator and a knowledgeable dance instructor. Months turned into years of dancing, learning and teaching. Eventually I was asked by a colleague who was opening a dance school to take the job of dance teacher trainer and to help new instructors put their passion and dedication into words.

Years turned into decades and I slowly I realized the impact my words were having on my students, performers, teacher trainees and colleagues. And one day a close friend told me: "Francisco, what are you waiting for? Write all of these down. Truly, these are *Words We Can Dance.*"

Living

*All human being come into this world as dancers.
But only the passionate, stubborn, rebellious,
illuminated or crazy ones
remain dancers throughout their lives.*

*The voice inside you that says: "Dance!"
is not your conscience. It's your life.*

*The light of a single dance
can illuminate a whole lifetime.*

*There is not a single problem in your life
that cannot be helped by dancing.*

*Dancing can help the person you are
to meet the person you want to be.*

*Enjoy life.
It would be sad if the epitaph on your tombstone read:
"Pity, I should have learned to dance."*

*We don't dance to escape life.
We dance to live life.*

*Nothing is as ephemeral as a dance
nor as eternal as its effects.*

*Dancers are never lonely.
In their hearts,
the whole universe is dancing with them.*

*Dancers live in a world of rhythm,
emotion and movement that vanishes
the moment they stop moving.*

*The floor is the dancer's canvas,
his body is his brush, life is his workshop
and his imagination his colors.*

*The day you leave this world,
you will do so with a smile
if you know you have danced enough.*

Learning

*Beginner, intermediate, advanced,
performance, competition, professional…
There are no small dance lessons.*

*It is possible to learn to dance without skill,
but not without desire and knowledge.* [1]

*You learn or teach with your mind.
You dance with your heart.
Your body is there just to show you
what you are thinking and feeling.* [2]

---
[1] Paraphrase of the Wright Brothers': "It is possible to fly without motors but not without knowledge and skill"
[2] Inspired by Johan Cruyff's: "You play football with your head. And your legs are there to help you."

Talent can't be seen, heard, smelled, tasted, bought, borrowed, copied, broken, stolen, killed or destroyed. It belongs in the same group of concepts as luck, destiny or unicorns; it doesn't exist! [3]

If you insist on using the word, talent is just another name for the desire to learn and improve.

When people claim to "see" talent, they are only seeing the effects of desire, perseverance and love.

---

[3] Inspired by Colonel Haldane's speech on luck in *The Intruders* by Stephen Coonts

If music is the arrangement of sounds and silences, dance is the combination of movement and stillness.

As a dancer you have to remember that you also are part of the orchestra.

When you dance, your goal is neither to dance to the music nor to dance on the music. Your goal is to be the music.

*We humans are always trying
to listen to our bodies;
but when we dance, it is our bodies that listen to us.*

*When it comes to dancing,
your mind may learn quicker
but your body will always learn better.*

*Every time you take a beginner class you see not just
what you missed the first time.
Your teacher also sees what he missed the first time.*

*Partner dancing is a team sport
and your partner is not your opposite
but your one and only teammate.*

*When you listen to your teacher,
your students or your partner;
keep your mouth tightly shut and your mind wide open.*

*In partner dancing no one
can ever be better than their partner.*

What a teacher calls a mistake in level one,
the same teacher will call it styling by level six.

When you set dance goals, don't be a copy,
not even of your role models.
There is nothing more wonderful in this life
than being different.

The day you dance exactly like your teacher
it means you have learned everything he knows.
Then is the time to learn everything else you can know.

*Question everything.
Especially your own questions.*

*Questioning what you assume to be true
will lead you to a clearer truth.*

*Your only stupid questions
are the ones you don't ask.*

*Your questions shape the way
your instructor teaches you as much as his answers
shape the way you dance.*

*You will never be in danger of making a mistake
if you are not willing to take the risk
of learning something new.*

*Those who risk nothing
are risking everything.*

*The friction of your dreams against reality
is what we call frustration.
It is not a sign of failure. It is a sign of change.*

Performing

School recital, wedding, half-time, club floor,
street fair, competition, Hollywood, Broadway…
There are no small shows either.

Showtime!
Break a leg, but please,
not on the stage stairs.

*Trophies and gold medals are not won on stage,
but on the rehearsal floor.
Competitions, on the other hand,
those are won deep in your heart.*

*We can assume the title
of expert teacher or performance champion
only when we admit to the fact that
we stand on the shoulders of giants.*

*Don't wait for the gold medal to be happy.
Be happy that you can compete.*

*Never assume you have an advantage
because you are the current champion.
Judges look at how you dance today,
not how you danced last week.*

*It is useless to triumph over your opponents
if you don't vanquish yourself.*

*Practice doesn't make perfect. Practice makes habit.
Practice and understanding make improvement.*

*Do not practice until you get it right.
Practice until you cannot remember
how to do it wrong.*

*Talent may sometimes dance with Luck.
But on any given night, the best couple on the floor are
Knowledge and Perseverance.*

"Failure is not an option!"
Now, that's a great plan for quitting.

*You will be a good performer
when you are able to love and respect
dancing, the audience and yourself in equal parts.*

*You are on stage doing that choreography
because nobody else in the world
can dance it quite the way you dance it.*

*Within minutes the crowd will forget
the steps you did on stage. But they will never forget
how your presence made them feel.*

*There are no small parts in group choreography.
If the last dancer in the rearmost line makes a mistake,
nobody looks at the lead dancer.*

On stage,
no matter how much more you want to do;
you can only dance
what your mind and body
know how to dance.

The day of the show
your dancing will not rise to the occasion.
It will simply default to your level of training. [4]

---

[4] Paraphrases of the Fighter Credo in *The Sixth Battle* by Barret Tillman.

If you want a career in dance,
I've got bad and good news for you:
The bad news: You will never finish learning.
And the good news: You will never finish learning.

Teaching

Dancing is an art.
Teaching dance is a science.

Teaching dance is the science
of pointing out the obvious.

In the profession of dance instruction
steps may be precious but ideas are priceless.

A successful dance lesson
is the one in which both student and teacher
have learned something.

*A good teacher will not impress his students
with his dancing skill.
But he will dazzle them
with their learning abilities.*

*Before challenging
the learning abilities of their students,
good instructors think about challenging
their own teaching abilities.*

*A lesson without a clear objective
is a failure even before it starts.*

*A dance teacher's most important objective
is to make the student aware of an improvement
between the beginning and the end of the lesson.*

*In a dance lesson the plan is often
the first victim of reality.*

*As a teacher,
anything you say in beginner class
can and will be held against you
in advanced class.* [5]

---
[5] Paraphrasing the Miranda Warning Card

In dancing there are no bad students.
There are only inefficient teachers.

Anybody can teach
a student with good abilities to dance.
A student without them needs a real teacher.

*Don't ever be afraid
to give away your knowledge.
If you are always learning,
you will never run out.*

*If someone "steals" your ideas,
remember that they cannot take from you
the most precious jewel of the treasure:
your creativity.*

*If you are teaching dance class
and your corrections
do not produce the expected result,
you are correcting the wrong mistake.*

*Your generosity, empathy and optimism
cannot be written in a teacher's resume,
but in class they are far more impressive
than trophies and gold medals.*

*An efficient teacher doesn't need to be patient,
because he knows that every part
of the teaching and learning process
has its proper time and place.*

*A good teacher doesn't need patience to teach.
Instead, he has to teach it to over eager students.*

Ever heard of the teaching rule of 1:100?
Every new idea you learn will allow you to teach a hundred students you could not teach before.

Never tell your dance students that you are going to work with them on this or that. Instead, tell them about this great new idea you are going to share with them.

*Be sure to teach your dance students
that which they already know.*

*If you dread teaching certain students raise your hand.
If your hand is up,
you also need to raise your training standards.*

*Keep talking to your dance students
about their future.
Especially if you want to have a future as a teacher.*

When you teach, don't guess.
If you want to look like a real teacher
you only get one chance to figure things out.

Intuition is a great tool,
but only when it is wielded
by knowledge and good intentions at the same time.

*It is fun to teach the advanced class,
but teach your beginners as if your life depended on it.
Because it does.*

*About ten percent of your dance students
will make elite performers or competitors.
The other ninety percent will make
your teaching career possible.*

Photo credits

Alfonso, Michael (unsplash.com) Page 16
Alvarado, Cesira (unsplash.com) Page 42
An, Liel (unsplash.com) Page 60
Baila Productions, École de Salsa Page 28
Cerullo, Danielle (unsplash.com) Page 55
Di Cristin, Lorenzo (unsplash.com) Page 69
Haste, Leart V. (pexels.com) Pages 34 and 48
Hoffman, David (unsplash.com) Pages 2, 12, 18, 23, 25 and 57
Fomenok, Vadim (unsplash.com) Page 20
Gouw, Tim (pexels.com) Front cover
Graham, Drew (unsplash.com) Page 6
Gupta, Pavan (unsplash.com) Page 52
Kepler, Jeff (unsplash.com) Page 40
Lumi, Ardian (unsplash.com) Page 67
Mcclean, Isaiah (unsplash.com) Page 8
Nikidinov (pixabay.com) Page 44
Oliveira, Hian (unsplash.com) Page 64
Pixelia (pixabay.com) Page 30
Rindao Rainier (unsplash.com) Page 62
Zittel, Michael (pexels.com) Page 38

About The Author

Francisco De La Calleja, author and blogger, is one of the most experienced latin dance instructors and dance teacher trainers in the Montreal (Canada) area. Although a salsa specialist, his dance experience ranges from Mexican folklore, ballet, ballet-jazz, ballroom and swing, to argentine tango, brazilian samba and even aerobics, dance fitness and rhythmic gymnastics.

He has taught over twenty-one thousand students in six different dance schools and has danced in, coached or choreographed for several dance troupes as well as movies, TV shows, sporting events, music videos and live performances including salsa Congresses in Montreal, Los Angeles, New York, Miami and Puerto Rico. He was a member of Salsa Team Canada from 2002 to 2005.

In 2015 he began a writing career which has yielded already two titles: *Words We Can Dance* and the soon to be released *She Dances Salsa… With Him!,* about the unspoken truths of learning, teaching and dancing Salsa. His next works, a compilation of dance teaching anecdotes and a training manual for Salsa and latin dance teachers are expected in late 2019 and early 2020.

You can learn more about his work and reach him through his website at www.shedanceswithhim.com

www.ingramcontent.com/pod-product-compliance
Lightning Source LLC
Chambersburg PA
CBHW041434010526
44118CB00002B/69